(Above) People raise their phones to take pictures of the legendary Manhattanhenge above 42nd street in New York. July 13, 2018.

A Note From The Publisher

There's an undeniable attraction many people feel towards the sun and moon. Part of that attraction is pure science—gravity—but I think the most interesting part, the part that speaks deeply to so many people, is the more emotional, and possibly spiritual, aspects of our sense of connectedness to those glowing orbs and bodies in the sky.

Earth-bound, here we are, all of us, constantly looking to the heavens for inspiration, or maybe a sense of smallness, or maybe that connection we feel when we see the sun or the moon in all their glorious granduer. Who isn't moved by the colors of sunrise or sunset? Who doesn't have fond memories of laying in the grass on a summer evening and absorbing the sense of peace that comes from looking at sky bursting with stars?

And on the topic of glorious granduer, New York is an endlessly beautiful and fascinating city. From its architecture, to its people, to its landmarks, it's a city that has perhaps been photographed as much, or more, than any other city in the history of photography. And, yes, as I write this I can almost hear Henri Cartier-Bresson and his fellow Parisian photographers voicing their boisterous objections to my statement.

Yet, in spite of the untold number of iconic photographs of New York that already exist, Gary Hershorn managed to find a way to show us his unique and spectacular vision of New York and her romance with the celestial bodies of the sun and moon.

For me, personally, I found editing this book to be a very peaceful, almost zen-like experience. It's rare to think of New York as either peaceful or zen-like but, here you have it, printed on the pages of this book is a peaceful, and zen, Big Apple. A city, and people, at one with the sun and moon.

Sincerely,
N. Warren Winter
Press Syndication Group

(Left) An almost full moon rising the night before the February super moon as seen from Hoboken, New Jersey. February 18, 2019.

(Next page) A super moon rising over lower Manhattan from Eagle Rock Reservation in West Orange, New Jersey. May 7, 2012.

Introduction

By Gary Hershorn

It began on a warm, spring evening in May 2012. News reports were announcing that a "Super Moon" (a term I'd never heard before) would be rising over New York City during the coming weekend. Intrigued, I decided it might make an interesting picture for the news agency I was working for at the time, Reuters. With the help of an app called LightTrac to track the moon's path in the sky, I picked a spot with spectacular views of New York City, Eagle Rock Reservation in West Orange, New Jersey. If the app was right, the moon would come up directly behind lower Manhattan.

As the moon began to rise behind One World Trade Center (which was still under construction at the time), I experienced my first "WOW" moment. 'Super Moon', indeed; the orb was huge, and several shades of orange, with the skyline accentuating its enormous scale. I snapped away, hoping that my camera lens would capture some of the beauty my eyes were taking in.

The photograph on the accompanying page created quite a discussion in the following days. It was published in media outlets around the world leading to questions about how the moon could be so big, how a photographer could know exactly where to stand to take this picture and how real the actual photograph was since the moon did seem overly supersized. I saw people talk about the photo on TV and read stories online; it was energizing as a photographer to see a single image discussed at such great lengths.

That night, a new celestial photographer was born.

When I took that Super Moon photograph, I was the lone professional photographer in that particular park. There were a few tourists nearby, most of them bemoaning the limitations of their mobile phone cameras, which were simply not equipped to capture the full scope of such a magnificent event. Now, when you go to the same spot on the night of a full moon, you are liable to be one of twenty or thirty professional or semi-professional photographers, all trying to capture the moon lining up perfectly with the Empire State, or the World Trade Center. The world's fascination with celestial events, especially over a city like New York, seems to grow with each passing day, especially when sharing them with the world (on platforms like Instagram) is so incredibly easy.

My fascination with the moon began when, as a 10-year-old kid, Apollo 8 blasted off in December 1968 with a mission to orbit the moon. The spectacle of a Saturn V rocket launch carrying humans to the moon was the coolest thing a kid could imagine. I vividly remember staring at the pictures that the world had never seen before, first the iconic earthrise taken from Apollo 8 and then the unforgettable Apollo 11 image of Neil Armstrong reflected in the visor of Buzz Aldrin while standing on the moon.

Then, in the summer of 2011 as the 10th anniversary of the 9/11 attacks on the World Trade Center approached, I began what has turned out to be a long term photographic project documenting the changing skyline of New York City. It was a summer filled with walking up and down the Hudson River in New Jersey looking for ways to show off to the world how New York City was finally getting back to being the great world city it always was. One World Trade Center was under construction and showing itself on the skyline of lower Manhattan and interest in New York City was high.

After I'd begun chasing full moons over New York City, it was a natural to then turn my camera towards the sun. Many mornings have been spent in all sorts of weather, watching the sun rising up behind New York City's amazing skyline; just as many evenings have been spent documenting a city awash in orange, red, pink or purple colors, as the sun drops out of the sky behind the Statue of Liberty, or the Brooklyn Bridge.

One might think that photographing the sun and the moon would be two very different things. In actual fact they are basically the same. As a photographer you try and find a spot that allows you to see either one as low on the horizon as possible where they are at their dullest moment of brightness and most full of color. Then, you have to wait; once the sun and the moon rise to a certain height they become very difficult to photograph. If you wait, then you can catch their descent back to the horizon.

And then, there's the clouds. Clouds can be either your greatest friend, or your most bitter enemy, when photographing celestial events. Some days, they shroud what you hope to see, frustrating your creative vision; but other times, they fill with color, dancing in the sunrise or sunset, creating an even more dramatic image.

Eight years into the project, New York is looking more magnificent than ever. As the skyline evolves, its new, taller buildings are enhanced by the incredible celestial events that take place over the city. Social media has provided a platform to share the beauty of New York with people the world over who either dream of coming to this city for the first time, or who are counting down the days to their next visit. I hope when people look at the pictures I share with them, they feel a connection to the greatest city in the world. And, the way I look at it, a shared interest in the celestial can only be a good thing. The recognition of how small, yet special, this little planet of our is, in the middle of the vastness of space, can lead us all towards treating it with a bit more care.

NEW YORK CELESTIAL

BY GARY HERSHORN

PSG

(Cover photograph) The Statue of Liberty is illuminated by the last moments of sunset as the moon rises in the east photographed from LIberty State Park in Jersey City, New

Full moon rising over lower Manhattan photographed from Jersey City. November 22, 2018.

For anyone who has watched my work over the years you will see two themes, silhouettes and people in motion. As a street photographer it is important to find your scene, or canvas, so-to-speak, and then have the patience to wait as people walk in and out of your frame.

This particular evening I was out with a couple friends walking along the Hudson River as we tried to find spots to shoot the moon rising behind lower Manhattan. It's easy to stand along the railing and shoot the moon; it is harder to find a way to add a human element to the scene. After stepping way back from the river I notice people were leaving a nearby office building which became the human element I was looking for.

I like working in layers; where a picture has a foreground element, a mid-dle element, and then something far in the background. This photo to me has two types of layering, one where you see the people, the skyline and the moon all working together but there is also an element of layering in the position of the people. I like when people in photographs are both moving in different directions and also are of different sizes creating that layering effect simply by being closer or farther from the camera. It is also important to me when people are in pictures of New York that they are in stride creating a feeling of perpetual motion through the city.

Moonrise over lower Manhattan as seen from Jersey City. March 19, 2019

(Left) Two women, illuminated by the warm glow of a setting sun, chat in a coffee shop window along 10th Avenue in Manhattan. February 13, 2019.

(Above) The sun reflects brightly off windows in lower Manhattan's financial district as a seagull stands defiantly on a railing in Hoboken. January 14, 2019.

The setting sun relects off an office window into Grand Central Terminal. February 26, 2019.

Information

People walk during sunset in the Vessel at the newly opened Hudson Yards in Manhattan. March 18, 2019.

(Above) A full moon rises above a skateboard park in Hoboken. November 21, 2018.

(Pages 18-19) The Hunters Moon rises behind lower Manhattan from Washington Rock Park in Green Brook Township, New Jersey, a vista that overlooks New York from 25 miles away. October 25, 2018.

(Right) The moon rises over midtown Manhattan and Hoboken photographed from Jersey City. October 22, 2018.

(Below) The moon rises above the Empire State Building. February 13, 2019.

(Page 22) Sunrise photographed from Liberty State Park. December 29, 2018.

(Page 23) Moonrise photographed from Liberty State Park. July 20, 2016.

The sun sets behind the Statue of Liberty photographed from the Manhattan Bridge with a large telephoto lens through the cables of the Brooklyn Bridge, February 5, 2019.

(Above) A goose is silhouetted in front of a moon rising over One World Trade Center photographed from the Newport neighborhood in Jersey City. June 25, 2018.

(Left) A seagull is photographed as the moon rises over New York. September 2, 2018.

A sequence of photos illustrate a full moon rising behind the Empire State Building as they loom large over a small residential neighborhood in Jersey City photographed from Newark, New Jersey. November 23, 2018.

In all my years of photographing in New York, nothing has surprised me more than the increased popularity of photographing "Manhattanhenge.

Manhattanhenge is a term created by astrophysicist Neil deGrasse Tyson and described on the site of the Hayden Planetarium as, "A special day (that) comes twice a year, when the setting Sun aligns precisely with the Manhattan street grid".

When I first started photographing Manhattanhenge there was barely a person who knew what it was let alone taking pictures of it. Over the years, the rise of social media has created what can only be described as a monster. On nights when it happens, that one day in late May and that one day in mid July, thousands of people now clog intersections across Manhattan bringing traffic to a standstill as everyone tries to capture an image of the sun setting perfectly along a street in Manhattan.

Views are best along the double wide streets of 14th, 34th, 42nd, and 57th. Bridges over 42nd Street will see people saving spots early in the morning for a sunset that happens around 8:15pm.

Manhattanhenge is one of the hardest celestial events to photograph in New York. With streets in shadow and shooting directly into the sun, nothing is easy about finding an exposure that brings it all together.

Whether you are shooting on a bridge, on the street with a wide lens showing the scene of the masses all with their phones held high or shooting with a telephoto lens along 42nd Street to silhouette people on a bridge with the sun behind them, you will experience a level of chaos that only a New Yorker would understand. *(continued on page 36)*

(Right) Sunrise aligns perfectly along 42nd Street in Manhattan photographed from Weehawken, New Jersey. January 19, 2016.

(Pages 32-33) The sun sets along 42nd Street as people celebrating Manhattanhenge stand on the Pershing Square bridge. July 13, 2016.

Manhattanhenge sunset down 42nd Street, shot from Pershing Square bridge. July 12, 2018.

Manhattanhendge sunset on 42nd Street. July 12, 2016.

(continued from page 30) Police do their best to get people out of the middle of the street. Pedestrians put their lives at risk by standing in the middle of streets with backs to oncoming traffic and taxi drivers shout obscenities out their windows as their cabs come to standstill for a few minutes as the sun sets. People outside of New York comment endlessly on social media posts wondering what the big deal is with another sunset.

To experience it is to understand it.

It is also an event that creates high disappointment in photographers when clouds sometimes obscure the sun. Years can go by without a Manhattanhenge actually happening.

Manhattanhenge also happens at sunrise in November and January. The beauty of a sunrise Manhattanhenge is that virtually no one knows it is happening so there is no chaos or people in the streets. Fewer people shoot photos so when they are published they are always a bit of a surprise to viewers.

It's best shot from New Jersey where you see the sun come up down 42nd street. Until recently, I would hardly see photographers out at 7am on a cold winter morning but this past January when I arrived to shoot the event moments before the sun started to rise, 30 photographers were already camped out on a street corner waiting.

There is no corresponding celestial event equivalent to Manhattanhenge with the moon, however once a year a full moon will make its way through a corridor of buildings, like the ones on 42nd Street when it rises looking similar to the sun when it sets.

The Strawberry full moon rises above 42nd Street, photographed from Weehawken. June 28, 2018.

(Pages 38-39) Ducks splash around in shallow waters of the Hudson River as the sun rises over New York Harbor photographed from Port Liberte, New Jersey. April 21, 2018.

$10,000
CASH REWARD

Moonrise over the Brooklyn Bridge. November 2, 2017.

Sunset on the High Line in Manhattan. October 26, 2017.

(Left) A crescent moon rises over lower Manhattan as haze from a forest fire in New Jersey colors the sky at sunrise photographed from Jersey City. March 31, 2019.

(Pages 44-45) The sun sets as seen from Brooklyn. October 31, 2016.

Another cool effect when shooting the sun rising behind lower Manhattan is to see what happens when it comes up directly behind One World Trade Center when photographed from a distance of anywhere from 8-12 miles.

Since the middle section of the building is unleased, there are no inner walls on these floors therefore it allows for the sun to appear to burn right through the building.

I noticed this happening a few years ago and tried and capture this for the week in November and the week in January when this happens. It is very important to make mental notes marking what happens at what times of the year so you don't forget. Of course unfavorable cloud conditions prevent pictures like this from being taken.

Sunrise behind One World Trade Center photographed from Arlington, New Jersey. December 8, 2018.

(Above) People photograph the sun setting out the window of the One World Observatory the night before a solar eclipse in New York. August 20, 2017.

(Right) People ride the ferry amidst the setting sun as they arrive at Battery Park after visiting the Statue of Liberty. December 5, 2015.

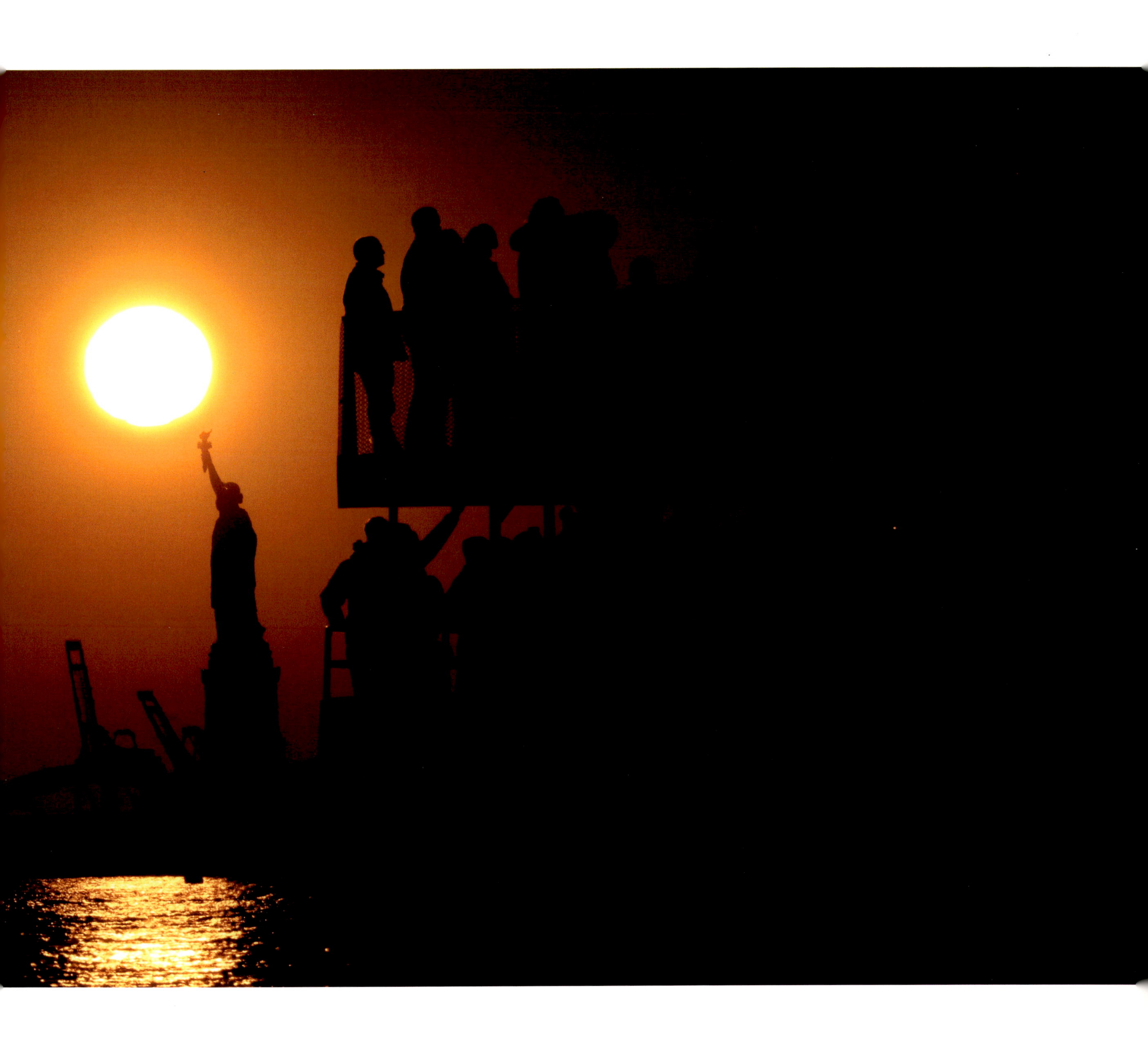

(Right) A red crescent moon setting as viewed from Brooklyn Bridge Park. September 23, 2017.

(Below) The moon rising photographed from Liberty State Park in Jersey City. June 11, 2017.

The sun rises behind One World Trade Center in lower Manhattan photographed from Jersey City. September 16, 2017.

(Right) Moonrise photographed from the South Street Seaport overlooking the Brooklyn, Manhattan, and Williamsburg Bridges crossing the East River. January 31, 2018.

(Below) A jogger at sunrise photographed from Hoboken. May 21, 2018.

(Above) The moon rising behind the communications antenna on top of One World Trade Center photographed from Jersey City. June 3, 2017.

(Right) The moon rises above a balloon in midtown Manhattan. September 27, 2017.

(Pages 58-59) Sunrise Manhattanhenge photographed from Weehawken with the Hudson River in the foreground. January 12, 2019.

Moonrise with the Empire State building lit in Christmas colors. December 24, 2018.

Moonrise with the Empire State Building lit in Thanksgiving colors. November 25, 2018

(Above) The moon rises over One World Trade Center photographed from Eagle Rock Reservation in West Orange, New Jersey. June 10, 2017.

(Right) The moon sets behind the Statue of Liberty photographed from Battery Park in lower Manhattan. July 8, 2017.

A crescent moon rises above 42nd Street before sunrise photographed from Weekhawken. January 8, 2016.

The moon rises behind the Empire State Building as people watch from Jersey City. September 28, 2015.

The sun sets behind the Manhattan and Brooklyn Bridges seen from the East River Park. The Statue of Liberty can be seen small on the horizon. February 2, 2019.

(Above) Moonrise over lower Manhattan photographed from Hoboken. November 27, 2018.

(Right) Moonrise over the Brooklyn Bridge. November 2, 2017.

The sun rises behind lower Manhattan as seen from Jersey City. March 11, 2019.

The moon rises at sunset behind lower Manhattan photographed from Jersey City. October 18, 2018.

As a photographer who likes to have people whenever possible to be in a picture of New York City, I realize it is far from easy to accomplish this every time. Certain times of the day and shooting from certain places make it virtually impossible to put people in every picture so my eye wandered to the sight of seagulls flying endlessly over the Hudson River.

Birds I feel add an element of grace and beauty to a photograph especially in their silhouetted form. Cityscapes need something to bring them to life or to humanize them. Using birds helps to play with perspective; the giant bird in New Jersey towering over the skyscrapers in Manhattan for example. Anytime I can make the city of New York look small compared to some form of life, I am at my happiest.

Seagulls, ducks and geese typically fill the skies at sunrise over the Hudson River as they head off for their daytime activities and return to base an hour or so before the sun sets. At certain times of the year, the setting sun perfectly illuminates the seagulls as the sit on railings next to the Hudson River around Hoboken, turning their white feathers a brilliant shade of orange and instantly making sunset recognizable in a photograph. Getting up close and personal is hard with seagulls but everyone once in awhile you encounter one that simply is not afraid of a human being. When you put a camera near their beak and they give you this quizzical look and you know instantly you have a picture that will make people laugh.

A bird is silhouetted as the sunrise rises behind the Empire State Building photographed from Hoboken. August 1, 2017.

The sun refracts through a window at the Whitney Museum of American Art in Manhattan. January 31, 2019.

The moon rises through the annual Tribute in Light as it is tested. September 7, 2017.

(Above) The Super Blood Wolf Moon begins to be eclipsed as it rises during a total lunar eclipse. January 20, 2019.

(Left) The moon rises behind One World Trade Center photographed from Jersey City. August 10, 2017.

(Page 78) A crescent moon rises above 6th Avenue before sunrise. October 6, 2018.

(Page 79) The moon rises through the Tear Drop 9/11 Memorial photographed in Bayonne, New Jersey. November 11, 2018.

A mother and daughter look on as the moon is partially eclipsed during a total lunar eclipse. September 28, 2015.

(Above) People stop on 14th Street to photograph the setting sun. June 26, 2017.

(Pages 82-83) The sun setting behind the Statue of Liberty. January 13, 2018.

The moon rises behind the Statue of Liberty from Liberty State Park in Jersey City. August 9, 2014.

The sun sets behind the Statue of Liberty as seen from One World Observatory. September 29, 2017.

(Left) Moonrise from the South Street Seaport with a view through the Brooklyn, Manhattan, and Williamsburg Bridges. January 31, 2018.

The Super Blood Wolf Moon eclipse over One World Trade Center. January 20, 2019.

A super moon setting at sunrise from Red Hook, Brooklyn. February 19, 2019.

(Left) The sun setting from Brooklyn Bridge Park. February 8, 2019.

(Right) The sun sets as seen from Battery Park at the southern tip of Manhattan. December 29, 2017.

The sun rises over the George Washington Bridge photographed from Fort Lee, New Jersey. December 31, 2017.

The moon rising over Manhattan and the Empire State Building as viewed from Pier C in Hoboken. February 18, 2019.

My multi-year project of photographing the changing skyline of New York can best be seen in photographs that contain multiple cranes in a single picture.

As new buildings emerge on the skyline the classic silhouette of Manhattan has been changed forever. Many people dislike the new look. Others will show a picture to friends and challenge them to name the city since New York is becoming so unrecognizable in new photographs that people say the skyline could be just about any city in the U.S. these days.

The cause of this is new buildings are going up so fast on the edges of the city, the iconic structures like the Empire State Building or Chrysler Building are no longer seen from many places they once were. Hudson Yards for example has done a great job of stealing the view of the Empire State Building from wide swaths of New Jersey. Angles that photographers used to shoot classic images from are no longer producing pictures that show New York off in all its glory.

This image of the Statue of Liberty shot from Port Liberte in New Jersey is particularly hard for me to look at. I see four cranes in Brooklyn whose positions mimic the arm of the Lady Liberty holding up her torch. Unfortunately, what was once a relatively flat perspective from this angle for shooting a sunrise or a moonrise behind the Statue of Liberty, is now a game of narrow angles forcing us to wait longer to see the sun and the moon as they rise over taller buildings. The longer you wait to see the sun and the moon rise the brighter they become making it harder to make a good photograph of them.

The new structures are eliminating potential pictures that photographers have shot for years. You expect to see these super tall buildings in Manhattan but seeing them go up in Brooklyn is a visual disappointment. As the angles narrow, so do the number of places available that produce interesting images. It is hugely important to be able to see the sun or the moon as low in the sky as possible to capture celestial events with their maximum color and, preferably right on the horizon when shot from a distance but the new development is taking these opportunities away from us.

The sun rises behind new buildings being constructed in Brooklyn photographed from Port LIberte. April 1, 2019.

Keith Kevin O'Connor
Colleen Ann
Paul Joshua Friedman
Marie Bernaerts-Kearns
V. Fersini Jr.
Frederick Rhodes
Jones II

(Above) The moon rising over Brooklyn. October 23, 2018.

(Left) Sunrise in the Empty Sky Memorial with One World Trade Center in the background photographed in Liberty State Park in Jersey City. September 11, 2013.

The setting sun reflects off the glass of One World Trade Center photographed through the Williamsburg Bridge. November 8, 2018.

The setting sun reflects off One World Trade Center as the moon rises. Photographed from Jersey City. August 4, 2017.

For me, nothing is better than a sunrise with swirling clouds in the sky. Blue sky sunrises and sunsets offer little drama and color, these are best photographed from a distance where you can show the size of the sun against the skyline of the city.

When the clouds are swirling and helping dim the sun's brightness as it gets higher in the sky, the lighting can be very dramatic as in this photo. The same effect can be seen on foggy mornings when the sun barely makes its appearance through the fog but silhouettes the skyline for maximum effect.

People are the key. It is important to find a low angle that allows you to put both the skyline of New York City and people together in the same image. People riding by on a bicycle work very well, as in this picture, because the low angle makes them appear much taller than those walking around them at the time.

To achieve a dramatic effect it is also important to ensure you are slightly underexposing the overall image so the outline of the sun is seen. This makes the clouds go black adding to the intensity of the image. This particular morning had clouds and some fog that helped shroud the sun and skyline. Exposure is a forgotten art I think in to-day's world of automatic exposures.

Sunrise from Jersey City. September 15, 2018.

A crescent moon setting behind One World Trade Center as seen from Williamsburg. January 30, 2017.

(Above) The sun above the Unisphere at Flushing Meadows, Queens. August 29, 2014.

(Pages 104-105) The sun rises through the clouds photographed from Jersey City. May 26, 2018.

The sun rises behind One World Trade Center photographed from Kearny, New Jersey. January 7, 2018.

A full moon sets in New York Harbor as seen from the Brooklyn Promenade. August 29, 2015.

(Above) Sunrise in New York photographed from Jersey City. March 11, 2019.

(Right) Sunrise in New York photographed from Hoboken. August 2, 2017.

The sun sets behind Lady Liberty photographed from Red Hook, Brooklyn. June 17, 2018.

A helicopter flies past as the sun sets behind the Brooklyn Bridge. November 10, 2017.

(Above) The moon over the Empire State Building as seen from Hoboken. January 13, 2017.

(Left) The moon rises over midtown Manhattan near the Chrysler Building and the Empire State Building photographed from Pier C in Hoboken. January 15, 2015.

A father and son watch the moon rise over lower Manhattan from Jersey City. June 25, 2018.

(Above) Geese are silhouetted in front of a moon rising over lower Manhattan as seen from Jersey City. August 23, 2018.

(Pages 116-117) The Statue of Liberty silhouetted at sunset in the New York Harbor. December 10, 2015.

(Below) Moonrise behind the Empire State Building from Pier A in Hobeken. November 16, 2016.

(Right) Super moon rising over lower Manhattan photographed from Washington Rock in Green Brook Township, New Jersey. February 19, 2019.

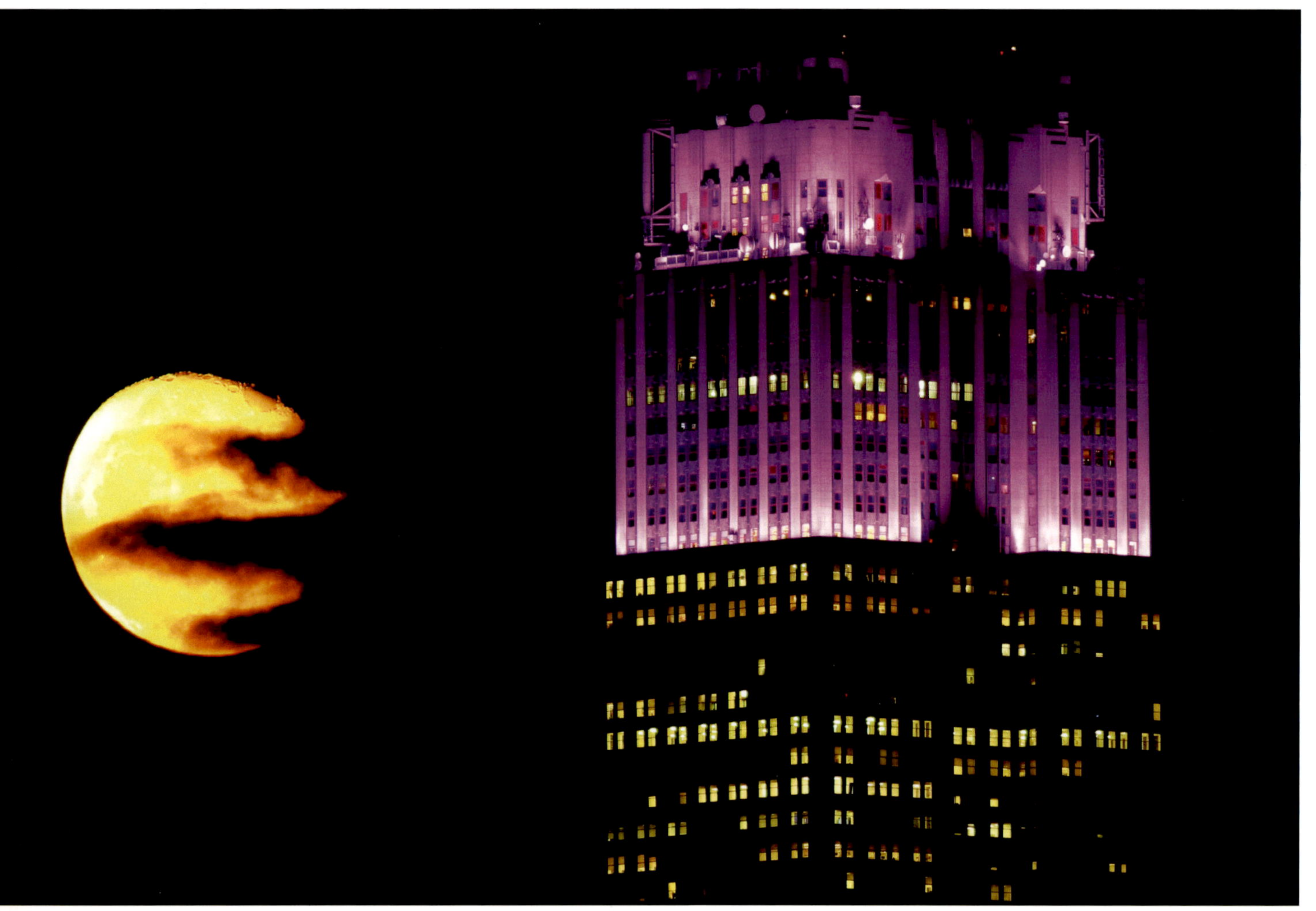

(Above) A father and daughter watch the moonrise over One World Trade Center as the sun sets behind them in Jersey City. August 23, 2018.

(Left) Moonrise at sunset photographed from Jersey City. December 10, 2016.

A low angle laying in the grasses of Liberty State Park as the moon rises above the Statue of Liberty. August 25, 2018.

(Above) People ride a ferry back to Battery Park as the setting sun turns the sky orange behind the Statue of Liberty. Novbember 21, 2017.

(Pages 124-125) Christmas Eve moonrise in New York photographed from Hoboken. December 24, 2018.

Geese fly over the Statue of Liberty as the sun rises as seen from Liberty State Park in Jersey City. December 29, 2018.

*Sunrise over midtown Manhattan viewed from Hoboken.
June 21, 2017.*

(Left) The moon rising behind the Empire State Building photographed from the High Line in Manhattan. November 23, 2015.

(Page 130) The sun rising behind the Empire State Building. May 26, 2018.

(Page 131) Moonrise in New York photographed from Jersey City. October 4, 2017.

(Below) The sun rises over Manhattan photographed from Eagle Rock Reservation in West Orange. February 17, 2019.

(Right) The sun sets behind the Statue of Liberty photographed from Battery Park. December 10, 2018.

(Pages 134-135) Moonrise over midtown Manhattan viewed from Eagle Rock Reservation in West Orange. August 8, 2017.

H&M

It always amazes me that when I talk to people at seminars and lectures about the moon rising in the sky. People often don't realize the moon rises every day. Nor do they realize the moon comes up 45 or so minutes later each successive day. Our eyes are trained to see the full moon rising around sunset but few people look up and notice the moon in the daytime sky.

For me, one of the best days to photograph the moon is the day before it's full. This is the day you can photograph the moon at the top of a tall building at almost the exact time the sun is setting creating a picture that shows moonrise and sunset in one frame. The moon has lots of detail in it so that it is not just a white dot in the sky and the buildings on the skyline will turn orange in the setting sun.

The picture on the right, and the one on page 4, were taken on the same evening about 20 minutes apart. It's easy to see how the moon gets brighter as it rises and the buildings on the skyline soak up the color of the sunset. At this hour the sky is still blue adding even more color to an already beautiful scene.

(Right) A full moon rises above the clouds behind the Chrysler Building and Empire State Building photographed from Pier C in Hoboken. February 18, 2019.

(Next page) An jet flies above Manhattan as the sun sets to the west photographed from the Arthur Ashe Stadium located at the Billie Jean King National Tennis Center in Flushing Meadows-Corona Park, Queens. September 6, 2016.

Sonnet 33

By William Shakespeare

Full many a glorious morning have I seen
Flatter the mountain tops with sovereign eye,
Kissing with golden face the meadows green,
Gilding pale streams with heavenly alchemy;
Anon permit the basest clouds to ride
With ugly rack on his celestial face,
And from the forlorn world his visage hide,
Stealing unseen to west with this disgrace:
Even so my sun one early morn did shine,
With all triumphant splendour on my brow;
But out, alack, he was but one hour mine,
The region cloud hath mask'd him from me now.
Yet him for this my love no whit disdaineth;
Suns of the world may stain when heaven's sun staineth.

A full moon rises above the Empire State Building photographed from Hoboken. February 18, 2019.

The Moon was but a Chin of Gold

By Emily Dickenson

The Moon was but a Chin of Gold
A Night or two ago—
And now she turns Her perfect Face
Upon the World below—

Her Forehead is of Amplest Blonde—
Her Cheek—a Beryl hewn—
Her Eye unto the Summer Dew
The likest I have known—

Her Lips of Amber never part—
But what must be the smile
Upon Her Friend she could confer
Were such Her Silver Will—

And what a privilege to be
But the remotest Star—
For Certainty She take Her Way
Beside Your Palace Door—

Her Bonnet is the Firmament—
The Universe—Her Shoe—
The Stars—the Trinkets at Her Belt—
Her Dimities—of Blue—

The moon rises at the tip of One World Trade Center's communications tower photographed from Jersey City. October 2, 2017.

Staten Island Ferry

Published by Press Syndication Group
2850 North Pulaski Road, Suite 9
Chicago, Illinois 60641

www.newyorkcelestial.com
+646.325.3221
sales@newyorkcelestial.com

Rights & Licensing Contact :
N. Warren Winter +646.325.3221
warren@psgwire.com

Editor, Publisher, and Designer : N. Warren Winter
Photographer : Gary Hershorn
Copy editor : Cara Winter

Both Gary Hershorn and N. Warren Winter would like to acknowledge the wonderful contributions of Steve Fine and Benedicte Lenoble for their help in editing this book.

The photographs that appear on pages 7 and 96 were reproduced courtesy of Reuters.

(Back cover photo) The sun is obscured by the moon behind the Empire State Building duing an eclipse photographed from 5th Avenue. August 21, 2017.

1st Edition, 2019.
ISBN 978-1-7323196-5-3
Printed in China

PSG